ROI: The sales person's secret weapon

First Published 2011
Revised and updated 2020

ISBN-13:978-1463764630
ISBN-10:1463764634

Derek Good
Auckland
New Zealand

Contents

Introduction

In 2020, a global pandemic changed the way many businesses operated. Employees went from a comfortable office-based environment to home based work and for some, the world fell out from beneath them. Many lost jobs, many businesses went under and purchasing was halted as organisations tightened their belts.

Now more than ever, the details and content of this book provide valuable insights into the best way to convince people to buy your products or services over your competitors. Times have changed but the principles remain the same. You need a convincing argument that puts your offering ahead of the competition.

During a recession, it can be harder to sell your products and services so having some tools to help you should be high on your list of priorities. We should never stop learning because when a big change happens like Covid-19, we may need to adapt quickly. If we don't adapt, we may lose out in ways that we never thought possible. If we aren't used to adapting or tweaking the way we do things, we may be too slow to react and someone will step in and we will be the ones missing out.

Consider what people need is times of hardship. How will your product or service take away some of the pain, move from a 'nice to have' to a necessity? Most of it is in the framing of the offering. This is what we will cover in this book; How to frame your offering so that it is convincing to your customers. Your job is to make your offering seem like a 'No Brainer'. They would have to be crazy not to go ahead. If you would like to know how to do that – then read on.

There are many opportunities to brush up on your sales techniques with books, online tutorials, articles and key tips from friends or mentors. I'm sure there is some great value in most of them. Let's face it; something's got to be pretty bad to be of no value at all. So, let me begin by telling you to build on those techniques and skills that you find work for you. Hold on to those aspects that you have had success with and make sure you continue to build on your own personal comfortable sales style.

This book is intended to give you something extra to add to your toolkit. Indeed, I feel that if you take this on board correctly it will bring you the opportunity to close deals and get commitments that you may not otherwise have realised.

Mine is not a brand new programme, a fancy acronym, a snazzy new widget or even a progression of something that is well known in the sales world. Rather, it is a simplistic approach that is so often missed in every area of business. Even if the whole world knew about the approach, it wouldn't harm your chances of selling. When I pitched the methodology to a well known worldwide electronics firm with its UK base in London, their reaction was one of, "Wow, why aren't we doing this?". They went further to say, "It's such a simple idea and has turned the way we do sales on its head. It's taking the customer view rather than our own".

As you can imagine, this buoyed my enthusiasm and confirmed how straight forward and sensible the approach is.

Most people are familiar with the traditional sales cycle. (See Fig 1.)

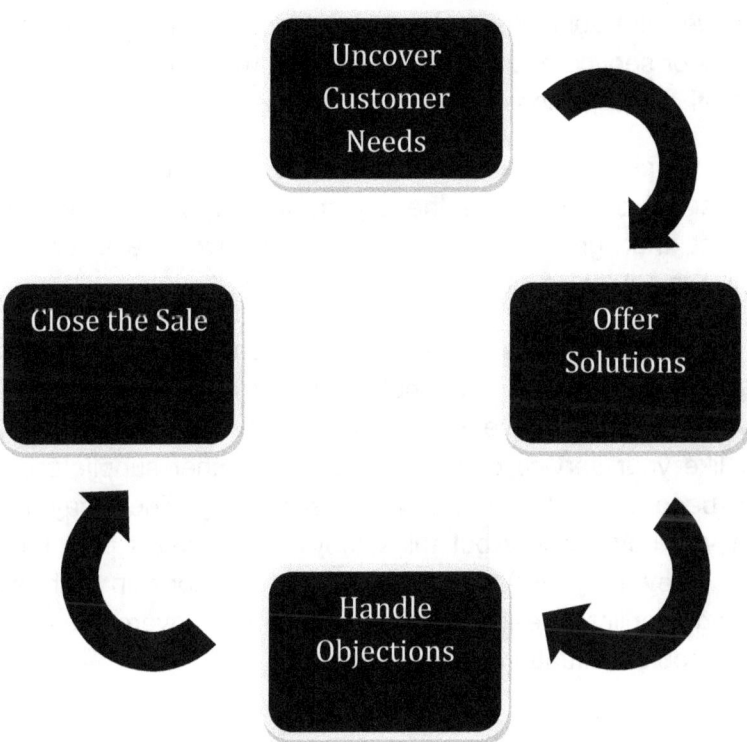

Fig 1: The Traditional Sales Cycle

The sales cycle is a useful reminder of the simple steps we should follow in our sales discussions. First and foremost, we need to understand our customer's needs. In this book, we are also going to extend this to identifying key needs or needs we can apply key benefits of our product or service to. We need to understand what presses our customer's buttons. What is their pain? What could we help take away for them? What will help them look or feel good? This is all part of the first step and is just as relevant for this approach as it is in sales generally.

Then we offer solutions and handle objections. If we know the product or service and the customer well, we should be able to head off any objections before they are raised.

Lastly, we close the sale. This is the commitment to go ahead. This is the signature on the paper, the order number, the contract, the agreement to proceed. You have to ask for this just like in any sales situation.

So much for the sales cycle. It's simple and it's necessary to understand it but things may not always go to plan. Customers may love what you have to offer but not have the money. They may like your service over and above the other suppliers but have been asked to get the cheapest offering. They may like what you have to say but think they'll never get it past their boss. They may already have a good relationship with an existing supplier. Great! This book can help you overcome all of these problem situations! Read on!

Value for money

All of us have a limit. For some it's quite low and for the tolerant others out there, it could be substantially more but there's always a limit. A limit for what you may ask. Well, let me explain. Suppose you bought a car one day – old or new – and you drove the car out of the car yard, the showroom or from wherever you picked it up from and 200 metres down the road it conked out and stopped running. What would you do? Right, you'd either walk back to the place you got it from (most of us would phone from a mobile device) and you would demand someone come and fix it, tow it, replace it or even suggest they do some unimaginable thing with it. We'd be a little upset but we'd be safe in the knowledge that for something like this, we'd be protected from losing out. We'd have a guarantee or a warranty of some sort. You certainly wouldn't get out of the car, slam the door and walk away mumbling that you'd be more careful next time you bought a car!

Let's say you were buying a piece of electrical equipment. DVD or Blu-ray players are fairly inexpensive these days but let's say you bought one brand new and took it home only to find that it didn't work. What would you do? Sure, you'd phone up the place you bought it from and ask them to replace it. You'd have a warranty of some sort and you'd want your $100 or whatever it was protected. You wouldn't just throw it away and hope for better luck next time.

Most of us have had a dreadful restaurant experience. Something didn't meet our expectations, the food, the service, the portion size, etc. Some of us will have complained and either asked for a discount, our money back or a replacement meal.

We have a natural tendency to ensure we don't get 'ripped off'. This translates in to us having our own monetary limit after which we will fight for our rights and make sure we get the value realised. For most of us, this limit is between $20 and $100. Anything more than that and we are more than likely on the offensive. Of course, it's different for different things. We may have a lower limit for something that comes with a guarantee and a higher limit for eating out but it's still going to be mostly in the band mentioned.

"So what?" you may be thinking. Well, I wanted to establish that personally most people have a pretty low limit before demanding value for their money. In business, people don't seem to have the same criteria. Business costs are sometimes expended without the same level of value required. If something doesn't quite work out or something doesn't have a quantifiable outcome, well the money has been spent and that's it. This is especially true of some 'soft' purchases like training or team building activities. One organisation explained to me once that they had just spent $250,000 on some management training but had no idea what they got for their money. What a classic! Now tell me, if that was your own personal money – would you hand it over without some sort of planned expectation or maybe a form of guarantee? Highly unlikely I'd venture to say. And yet in the business world, money often changes hands for vast sums without any real value explained, gained or even expected.

So, what's this got to do with you as a sales person? Well, it's an edge, a point of difference that can help you beat the competition. In fact, it could be the missing piece to a number of puzzles. Firstly, the people you are trying to sell to often would like to go ahead but they need to convince someone else to part with the money. Secondly, your proposal may be very similar to the next one and you may lose out on price, history, quality, safety or a host of other reasons – a decision often made on what seems to be the toss of a coin. If you can help your offering become a 'no brainer' then the person giving the go ahead would be crazy not to buy from you. That's the point. Stop worrying about trying to sell and get them to buy. By the time you've finished this book, you'll have a fresh set of ideas that will help you improve your performance as a sales person because you will be able to unlock a door that most people didn't even know had a key.

ROI – the basics

For us to prepare for the kicker in this whole concept of giving you the edge in your industry, we need to look at a few basics. The term ROI or Return on Investment is a buzz phrase in certain business circles. In fact it is often termed ROE or Return on Expectation where you set out a set of outcomes expected and measure against them. ROI though has a connotation that you are putting something in (Investment) and you expect something out (Return). Indeed, if you don't know what the return is, then the investment part isn't an investment at all, it's a cost! And costs are expenses or necessary expenditures that people want to keep as low as possible.

To understand the very basic component is to use the formula:

This gives us the Net Gain in a situation. Basically Net Gain is the amount we are left with after taking the total costs away from the total benefits we receive. We account for the costs and work out the value of the benefits. To turn this into an ROI percentage, we divide the net gain by the costs and multiply by 100% as follows:

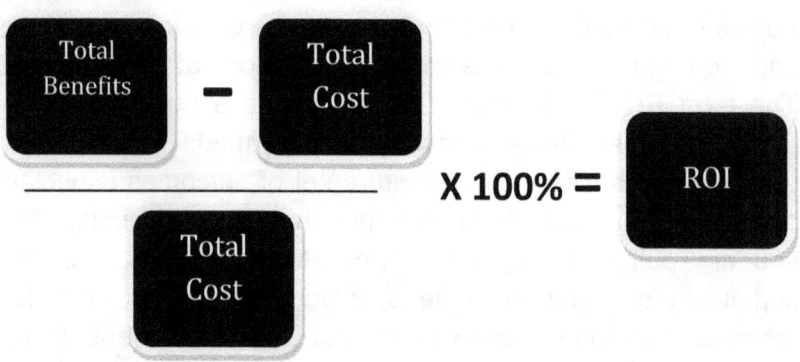

As an example, let's say that something is costing us $10,000. For this initial example, it doesn't matter what it is, we're just working on the maths and need the formula to do so.

For our investment of $10,000, let's say we have predicted $40,000 worth of benefits. Don't worry about how we got that figure yet, we're just working on the maths. So, using the two formulas above, we know that our net gain will be:

And according to our ROI formula from the page before, we therefore also know that our ROI will be:

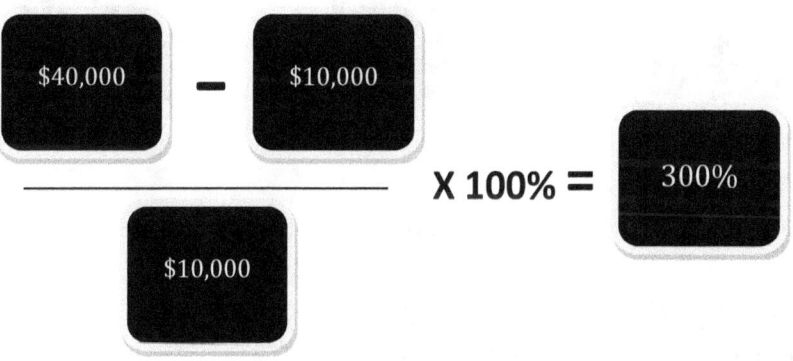

So, a 300% return in this case sounds pretty good. You wouldn't mind receiving a 30% pay rise for example, so a return of 300% would be very attractive.

Okay, one more to make sure we have this. Let's say we have worked out that we will receive a total benefit valued at $50,000 for an investment of some new hardware. We also have worked out that the new hardware plus installation and training costs plus a bit of lost time for the employees etc amounts to $20,000 in total. So, with our two formulas, we firstly know that our net gain will be:

| Total Benefits | **–** | Total Cost | **=** | Net Gain |

Or namely for this example:

| $50,000 | **–** | $20,000 | **=** | $30,000 |

And our ROI expressed as a percentage is:

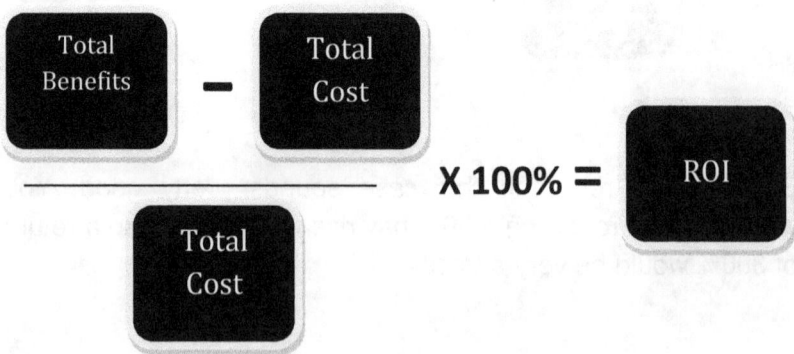

$$\frac{\text{Total Benefits} - \text{Total Cost}}{\text{Total Cost}} \times 100\% = \text{ROI}$$

Or namely for this example is:

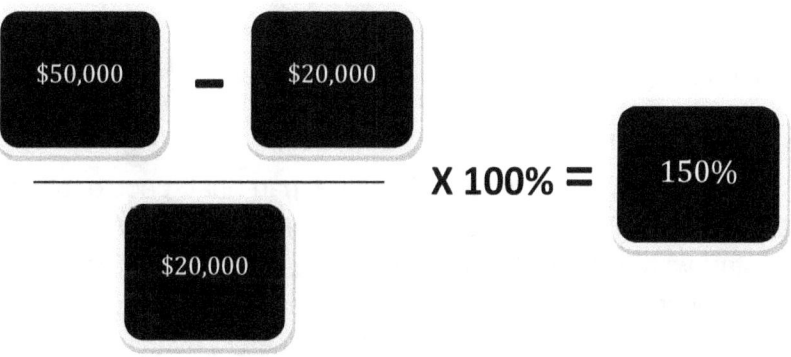

The maths should be quite simple. If you're still struggling, take a bit of time later to run through it again. If maths isn't your strong suit, then ask for a bit of help from a friend. This is about as basic and as complicated as it needs to get though, so I hope you're still with me. If this was laboriously slow for you, I apologise and let's get moving.

Investment

Let me share a point on working out the investment. This is not only the capital expenditure. Many people forget the wages and time of those employed to implement the investment, the loss of sales for example for time someone may be out of action and perhaps the additional cost of getting people up to speed. The true amount should be calculated to identify the real amount that will be required to buy, implement or generate the investment. However, you shouldn't get too bogged down in working everything out to the last dollar. People can spend thousands of dollars working on a return on investment calculation only to discover it isn't worth doing it. Consider taking a high level view first. It should take you minutes or even seconds. Then if the figures seem to stack up you can be a bit more detailed in your calculations.

Return

The return on the investment is the part that people often struggle with. That's the part that is essential though. Where do we start with this? Well it's quite simple. We firstly list down all the potential benefits that could be realised as a result of the investment. Write down anything that comes to mind in the first instance – throw nothing out. This is a brainstorming exercise. In brainstorming, we don't cull anything or we will stem the flow of ideas and suggestions. To get a good idea, you need lots of ideas. This is a good time to invite others to assist you in the brainstorming session. What we are trying to identify in the return first comes as 'identified benefits' from whatever it is we plan to implement. At this stage, we aren't looking at monetary value – we are just trying to identify descriptive benefits.

Let's look at an example:

Let's say we are buying a new computer. What will be the benefits over our current position (i.e. we currently have an old, somewhat unreliable computer)?

1. Reduced down-time from crashing

2. Faster operation of programmes

3. More compatibility of modern software

4. Feel better because we have something new.

Okay, so we have listed just four benefits and could have listed many more. For our basic example though, we have identified these as areas we feel will benefit us most. For each of these we then look at how we can assign a monetary value:

1. Reduced downtime from crashing – let's say we estimate that on a daily basis, the current computer crashes twice and each time it takes 15 minutes of our time to re-boot and open up everything we were working on. Okay – so that's 30 minutes a day which is 2 ½ hours a week or the equivalent of a day a month!! If your salary is $5000 a month and 1/20th is lost on computer crashing – that's $250 a month you can save just from the computer crashes.

2. Faster operation of programmes – this may take a bit more to work out. But let's say the new processor allows our operation to improve our productivity by 15 minutes a day – well, that's 5 hours a month (.25 hours x 20 working days) – let's say half a day a month. At the salary we started at, that's $125 a month on productivity for faster operation.

3. More compatibility of modern software – again, this can be tricky to identify. The old machine may not be able to support more efficient, faster software. You would have to specifically find something to make the point and you may do so and work out a brief calculation to make your case stronger. In our case let's just leave it as a possibility.

4. Feel better because we have something new – there's no doubt everyone works a little more productively when their morale is up. Getting a new computer is one way to boost morale. You can work on some productivity

figures like an increase in output by 2% and from that you can identify what that means in terms of your salary or your production. For us though, we'll leave it at zero.

Now, when you add these benefits together, you can see that in just one month, you have identified $375 of saved time alone. If the computer is going to cost you say $1500 including installation, then you have the formula you can use. $375 per month x 12 months for the first year = $4500. So our cost is $1500 to buy it and our total benefit is $4500 for year one:

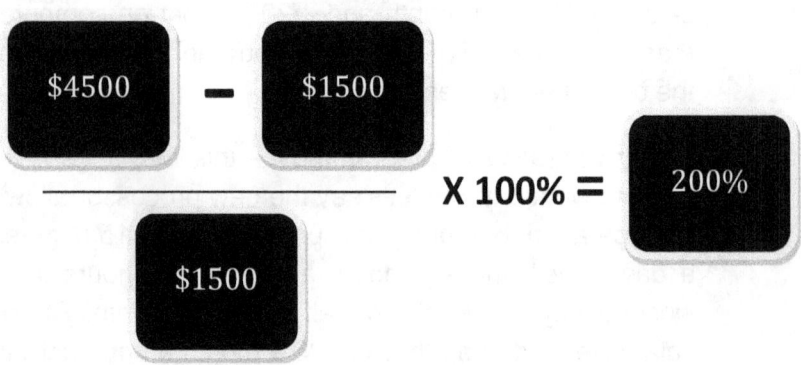

So, we have shown that in 12 months, we can demonstrate an ROI of 200% PLUS we'll have a machine that is compatible with up-to-date software and we'll feel better because we have a new computer. Notice, we don't justify getting a new computer because it will help us feel better – rather we describe that as a bonus. We can completely justify the new computer through logical steps. Here's where you can turn the emotional purchasing of 'Make you feel better' on its head. Logical purchasing is longer lasting and easier to justify (more of that later).

You can also see that as well as showing an ROI percentage you can work out how long it will take to get your money back (the payback period). In this case, we know it's saving us $375 per month and costing us $1500 all up. So, our payback period is:

$1500 Total / $375 (savings per month) = 4 months.

This is also a useful argument for when you sell your product / service to your customers. They may want to know the payback period. Again, we have kept this pretty simple and high level but it's also pretty convincing.

Okay – so that's the basics of ROI. It is important to be familiar with that part before we get in to the approach for using it as a sales person. There are plenty of help books and free formulas you can download on the topic. I can recommend further reading in this area from our book, "Return on Investment Made Easy" – details at the back of this book.

For now though, I hope you have grasped enough of the basics to see that ROI predictions are about identifying benefits and converting the benefits into monetary terms.

What's next? Well now, we need to apply these principles to you as the sales person. Let's read on!

Key benefits

When you are thinking about all the benefits your organisation, product or service has you also need to start thinking of some of the points of difference that your offering may have over the competition – let's call these 'key benefits' or benefits that may set you apart from others. You may have heard of the term USP – Unique Selling Proposition. This is the one thing that sets you apart from the competition. Just take a moment and think about your product or service or company itself. What sets you apart from the competition? We're not just talking about price, quality or service here. We need to go deeper. Specific things that you can provide that you know outstrip the competition. One of those big three may be where you focus but you'll need to list some specifics. A very important aspect of being a great sales person is to know your competition. Understand what they offer and how you can use that to your advantage. You don't want to be in a meeting with a client and try to sell them on a benefit you have only to be told that one of your competitors has a similar benefit and it's a bit better than yours!

Let's look at a few examples:

Insurance

Some of the benefits you can list from car insurance could include:

- Peace of mind
- Low excess in case of accident
- No-claims bonus
- Free windscreen replacement cover
- Lower premiums for drivers over 25
- Group insurance for more than one vehicle
- Named driver insurance options
- Two month non-payment grace period.

These are just some examples. Now, let's say you are the sales person of that insurance policy and you are aware that the unique benefit that you have is the fact that you offer a no-claims bonus higher than your competitors. This would be termed **a key benefit,** especially if the rest of the benefits are what people can get from the other insurance companies.

Okay, so we have our list of benefits. Well, these aren't really benefits yet, they're more like features. Features are first level views of reasons to go ahead. They may or may not be a benefit to the customer yet. You know the sort of thing. A mobile phone may have many features like a 10 mega pixel camera, option to make video calls and ability to retrieve and send emails. All great features....if you need them. If you don't need them or use them, these are purely features that provide you with no benefits. A true benefit is something you get as a result of using a feature. For example, if you used the mobile phone to retrieve emails, a benefit could be that you save time in getting back to customers as you don't have to wait until you are back in the office. You may not lose the job, because of your quick response. How many jobs not lost would pay for the benefit of having this new feature available to you?

One way to understand if a feature is really a true benefit is to take things a little further and ask the 'So what?' question. We'll do that in the following chapter. For now, we're keen to get the benefits out on the table.

Let's take another example:

Mobile phone plan

Some of the benefits you can list from a mobile phone plan could include:

- Reduced calling rates to certain numbers
- Free weekend calls
- Unlimited texts
- Low mobile to landline rates
- Free phone unit
- Free upgrade phone after 12 months
- Free data usage
- Low rates to users on the same network.

Again, we have created a quick list of benefits. We can go on and make a bigger list if we like. Remember: don't throw anything out at this point. Let's say that a key benefit and the USP for this example company is the free upgrade phone after 12 months. This key benefit you can play off against all the other companies because you're the only one that provides it. What you need to do is help the customer identify what this means for them. It may mean the following:

- Access to new technology within 12 months without having to pay more money
- Less likelihood of breaking down or even breaking apart
- Improved battery life with a new model
- The feel good factor of a new mobile phone every 12 months rather than 24 or 36.

You need to know your customer in order to help them see the real value of these key benefits. If you start throwing these in the direction of your customer without knowing what pushes their buttons, you're not going to impress anyone. However, the minute you get the right pressure points you will have nailed it.

Let's take an example of manufacturing goods:

Commercial Fluorescent Light Fittings

Some of the benefits you can list from your particular company offerings could include:

- Free lighting design service
- Customised light fitting design
- Fast turn around
- Easy access to the company owners
- Access to visit the production facility

- Products manufactured in this country
- 20 year guarantee on products.

So, we have created our list of benefits for the company. Notice here, we haven't gone into the benefits of the particular products in this example. We have chosen to offer company benefits. This may be the direction to go in if you really can't provide discernible benefits compared to the other competitors in the market from a product perspective.

Again, we could analyse each benefit for its inherent value and try to sell on each of them. What we have learned however, is that if a benefit is not required by a customer then it isn't a benefit it's just a feature. Let's say we felt our lighting design service was excellent and for goodness sake – it's free!! If the customer has its own lighting design team and prides itself in doing their design for their customers they may not be impressed. In fact, that sort of lost argument may prompt them to negotiate a discount if they do their own design.

Going back to the sales cycle, we need to understand our customer's needs. If we know for example that your customers are 'pro local made' you could use that as a lead in or as a bonus. It's not something that would normally swing an order your way but it is something that will tip the scales. It's a bonus item. So tuck that away and have it ready.

The key benefit that may set you apart here may be the fast turn around. Let's say competitors normally run a six-week delivery and you can offer products within a week. If the customer is one that doesn't get a long lead time themselves, this can swing it. You can start examining the benefits to them. Ask the questions, "How will this help them? What pain will this take away?" Build your sales case based on these types of principles. Have something in your argument like, "Having the ability to have products delivered within a week means you will save time on installation costs because you won't have to go back to sites to fit the lighting if they arrive late." If the customer knows they build in two extra days because they can't guarantee the delivery and you can fix it for them, how much is two extra days worth to them? Again, use the argument that if that happens on every job and they do fifty jobs a year, that saving could pay for their fleet for three months. It's such a powerful argument because it's taking away one of their bills. Remember, you are highlighting a bill they have to pay and the longer they leave it, the more money they are wasting.

Once you have sold them on the idea, throw in a bonus for them like, "And because our products are all manufactured in this country, you're supporting local industry and jobs". That will only confirm things for them and add an emotional element to the logical purchase decision.

If this was your business and these were the seven major benefits you can derive from your organisation, you can start working on the benefit-to-customer for each of them. As they stand they are just features. You turn them into benefits by relating them to the needs of the customers you have. The first step though is to work through the types of benefits they may be to your types of customers. This is most of the work. Do it once and it's done. Once you have then picked key benefits for certain customers a few times, it will be easy to do all the time.

HINT: It may be that your company brand has inherent key benefits. It's not always the product or service. Sometimes it's the brand itself. Having a brand with a great name may indeed sell itself. However, if you come cross a great sales person as a competitor, you better have more than just the name of the brand as you'll see later on.

So what?

The title of this chapter sounds a bit odd doesn't it? So what? It's meant to ensure that we have thought things through. Have we taken things to the next level and understood the real value because if we haven't, someone will be asking the 'So What?' question. It means we have asked the question of ourselves before someone else does.

Let's take each of the benefits from our first example and apply the 'So What?' test.

The car insurance policy was supposed to give us the following:

Peace of mind. So what? So that if we do have a car accident we know that we are covered with insurance. So what? So that if there's damage to another person's car or our own, we won't have to pay the whole bill. So what? So even if we hit a Ferrari, we only have to worry about the excess. Okay, so now it's starting to mean something to us. We're thinking about some bad scenarios and we're feeling better about the fact that we do indeed have some piece of mind. We have not stopped asking the 'So what?' question until it gives us something of meaning. Let's continue with our list.

Low excess in case of accident. So what? So that if we do have an accident, the amount of money we have to pay is lower than other policies. So what? Well, compared to other policies, this means you pay only half the amount. So what? So you don't have to reserve as much for that occurrence as you would normally do and free up some more cash. Okay – sounds good.

No claims bonus. So what? So if you don't make a claim, your premiums reduce every year. So what? So you save money. Okay – sounds good.

Free windscreen replacement cover. So what? So you don't pay to replace a windscreen if it gets cracked or chipped and it doesn't affect your claims bonus. So what? So if you're driving down the road and a rock hits your windscreen and cracks it, you can get it replaced free of charge and save hundreds of dollars. Okay – sounds good.

Why don't you have a go yourself at the other items on the list? Ask the 'So What?' question until you can say, "Okay – sounds good."

- Lower premiums for drivers over 25
- Group insurance for more than one vehicle
- Named driver insurance options
- Two month non-payment grace period.

Make it real

What can really add value to your sales pitch is if you can help the customer see what the saving or benefit means in real terms. For example, if you can point out that the saving from the benefit you offer will pay for their rent for six months or pay for their secretarial staff for a year, it suddenly has concrete meaning and tangible benefits. Again, you need to know the sort of money your customer is paying for these things. You can find out by asking or start to work out some key figures for expenses for companies and be prepared – they may not even know themselves. Find out what they hate paying for and give them the good news that really you're going to pay it for them from the savings you're going to help them make by buying your product or service.

Help the customer see that the savings aren't just going to be an amount on a bank statement or some wispy amount that nobody will ever see the benefit of. Latch on to something that has meaning and value to them. Imagine if someone said to you that all your fuel bills for a year will be paid for or your groceries will be free of charge for six months. That's an attractive proposition because those expenses are necessary and often begrudgingly spent.

If you can take away that pain somewhat by showing them that they can effectively save that money by what you're providing as well as cover the cost of what you're offering. It's really a decision that is easy to make – a 'no brainer' in effect.

No brainer

We've all heard the term. If something is a 'no brainer' it's basically an easy decision. You don't have to use any brain power to work out that you should go ahead. If somebody said, give me ten dollars and I'll give you hundred straight back and held it out to show you, you'd probably ask, 'What's the catch?' But if they signed you a guarantee that all you needed to do was hand them the money and that as you handed it over, they would hand the hundred over in the other hand at the same time, it would really be a 'no brainer.'

Many sales opportunities are lost because the customer actually makes no decision. They don't see a compelling enough argument to go ahead. They aren't convinced so they hesitate, deliberate further or just hold off because they can't see the quantifiable reason to act. In fact, findings by Thomas & Company Incorporated* showed that of over 700 proposals that were presented, 55% were listed as no decision / pending. Eventually only 2% of those 'no decisions' were turned into a sale. The remaining 98% were lost. In this example, the sales people were spending over half their time trying to sell a service to a prospective client that won't buy.

*This data is available from www.evancarmichael.com where a similar study by customer centric systems was referred to as showing that between 60-80% of all prospects or customer losses are due to 'No Decision.' Like all techniques, I strongly encourage further study to develop your skill and confidence and referring to this website and others will be well worth your while.

Sometimes the prospective customer throws up excuses for not making a decision. You can help cut through these excuses by helping them see a compelling case to go ahead. Organisations tend to spend the money on something even if it isn't with a competitor in your field, they will invest it in something. These days you are not just competing with the other companies in your field, you're competing with every other organisation out there that has a product or service to sell. If you're selling software, someone selling hardware could take the budget you're after. If you're selling training, then you are also competing against someone selling interior design or furniture. Organisations have limited funds and whoever can provide the most compelling argument to go ahead because of the amazing benefits will get the best chance of taking the budget.

If you can make your offering such a compelling business proposition, you may even create a budget out of nothing. You know the sort of logic – if you can't afford the extra rent but you decide to quit smoking, there's the money for the extra rent.

No brainers are the key to helping prospective customers or existing customers agree to the sale. In fact – help them want to 'buy' rather than be sold to. Create some added tension by declaring that you only have enough for three customers or a limited time to get on board. If these tactics are plausible, real and can be substantiated, then they add even more weight. I'm not talking about the high pressure sales techniques of 'time share' sales as an example but real, limited opportunities that still allow the customer to be in charge, feel in control and able to use their decision making preferences.

Incumbents

One of the issues sales people will face is the fact that the customer already has a supplier. This represents an incumbent scenario. An incumbent is the existing supplier to the customer and often has a strong relationship built on emotional reasons. This can be very daunting to a sales person wishing to convert the customer to them. Having a robust ROI discussion can help to reduce the value of the emotional ties to the incumbent and provide analytical information such as insight into financial gains and returns which will assist the customer in logical decision making. Making a strong ROI argument for the customer that he will be able to reduce his own resources or upfront investment can sway them your way.

Quantifiable data example

Here's an example of how quantifiable ROI data can be used.

A government contact centre with 400 staff is looking to reduce costs. One of the highlighted areas is Call Handling time. In a contact centre, there are costs associated for every second an agent is on the phone. These costs include the agent's salary, the costs of overheads, the free phone number, managers, hierarchy etc. The average Call Handing time in this organisation is 8 minutes. The target is to reduce the Call Handling time to 7 minutes.

If the cost for a minute of call time is $50 and they take 20,000 calls a month, then effectively, you can save them $1,000,000 per month ($50 x 20,000)! If you also know how much it will cost them to reduce that call time including cost of training for all staff and managers, salary based on time to be trained away from their workloads etc, you can provide a ROI calculation.

In this example the company has 400 staff members and everyone needs to go on a one day training course to be given some Call Handling techniques. The managers also need two days to be trained on effective coaching methods to keep the programme sustainable and to put a coaching regime in place to maintain the results. The company already has time allocated for coaching but the additional training will help to focus on improving the coaching effects. The maths look something like this:

- 400 staff x 1 day x $600 per day (cost of salaries, overheads etc) = **$240,000**

- 40 managers x 2 days x $900 per day = **$72,000**

- Cost of training by the provider = **$200,000.**

Total cost = $240,000 + $72,000 + $200,000 = **$512,000.**

Using our formula for ROI:

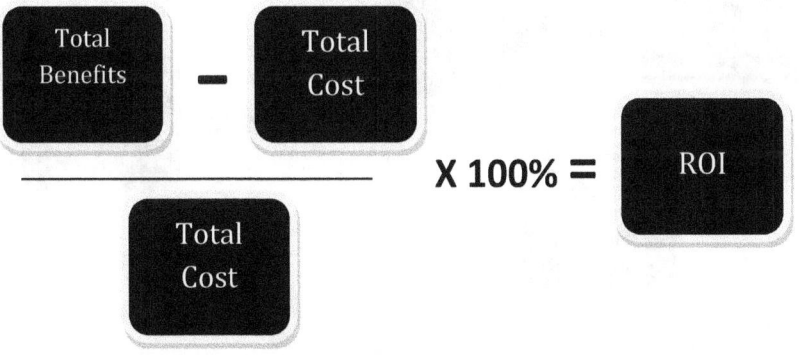

We can see:

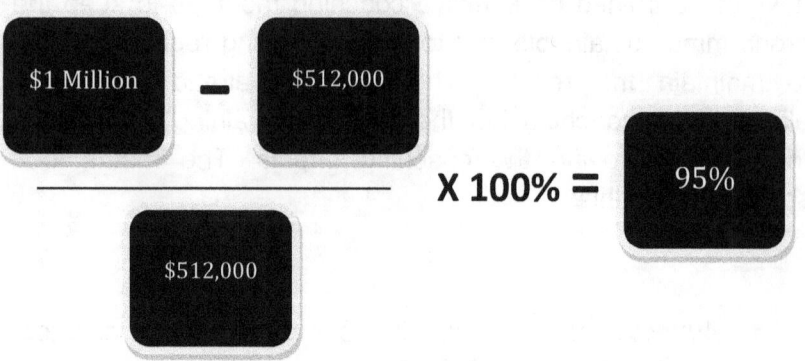

So, within one month of completion, the company had already made its money back. Based on a 12 month period, the rough figures (not taking into account depreciation costs etc) would be even more impressive:

Over a 12 month period, with the same savings per month:

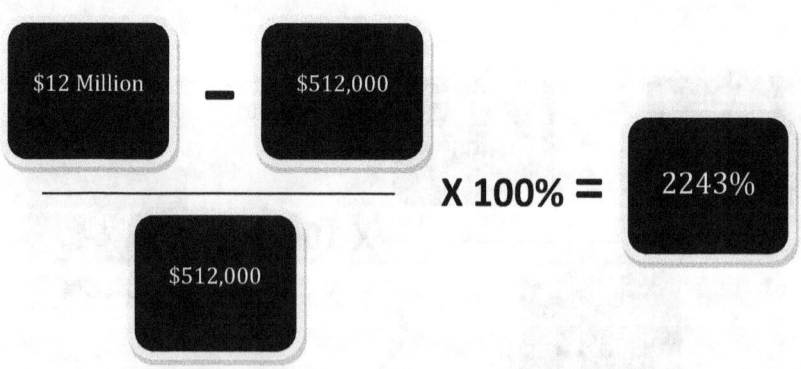

In this example, the figures look impressive – even too impressive – a 'no brainer' for sure. However, this gives you as the sales person some leeway to actually make it even more of a no brainer. There's no real disputing of the figures, but let's say you throw into the conversation something like, "We're very confident in the abilities of our organisation to achieve these results. However, let's say you only achieved half of what we see here. Let's say we only reduce the call handling time by 30 seconds, that's still 1100% ROI and a break even after a little over one month".

Your argument becomes pretty persuasive when you enter this discussion about 'likelihood of results'.

Likelihood of results

This is the discussion about reducing the expectation and talking about the possibilities of achieving a portion of the expected result. Even if your figures stack up pretty well, you can often tip the scales by showing that even by getting half the expectation, it's worth going ahead. Or you can say something like the following as an example, "Although we're aiming for a 30% increase in your sales through this new intervention, we have never seen less than a 20% increase in every single case we've had". Wow! That's powerful and especially believable if you have data to back that up. It's not about trying to convince someone of the one option you have on paper, it's about helping them see that other outcomes are possible and to see the benefits of those outcomes too.

Of course, you could blow them out of the water if you were to explain for example that even though the target is to increase customer retention by 30%, you could double it or even more. Help the customer see that the possibilities are bounded only by their imagination or own restrictions.

Make your customer look good

As a sales person talking about ROI and working with figures, you need to keep it as simple as possible. If people don't understand it, they won't be convinced by it. If they find it too difficult, they'll defer a decision or say no. If they are made to look incompetent, they'll back away.

Bear in mind that one of the key aspects of your role is to help the buyer look good. Help them to save money or make money. Help them to do their job which is to 'Buy' from you. Nobody likes being sold to – they want to buy. Make it easy for them by keeping it simple as well as showing them that it all adds up.

In some industries, there is a 'safe bet', a company that everyone knows and that has a good reputation for product or service. In the computer industry in the 80s it was IBM. The saying went, "Nobody got fired for buying IBM", meaning that if you went with IBM and there was a problem, it would be okay because they were the most reliable and highly reputable computer company of their day. Similarly in the UK commercial lighting market, "Nobody got fired for buying Thorn Lighting", because they were the 'safe bet' and highly reputable. When I was selling commercial lighting in the 90s, it was sometimes hard selling against Thorn because of their reputation. I had to have a more compelling reason for people to buy the products I was selling.

In some cases, your customer will be tempted to stay with the 'safe bet' because they know there won't be any issues if something goes wrong. However, if they buy from your organisation (if it's not the safe bet) and something goes wrong, they have to answer for their buying decision.

Your argument needs to be pretty water tight for them to feel safe. Can you offer them a guarantee or some sort of agreement that states you will ensure they get what they are promised or you will work for free until they do? Help them to feel safe in buying what you're selling. It is likely they will feel secure when you have shown them the financial benefits through your ROI calculations.

Elevator pitch & your offerings

Okay, you've seen a few examples. Now let's look at your company, its products or services. Grab some paper and a pen – we'll wait for you.

Ready?

Okay. Firstly, define what it is you do. This is your elevator pitch. How would you define what you do to a stranger in the twenty or so seconds you may share in a lift? For clues on this, refer to the company vision statement, business plan, website, brochures, etc. Somewhere, this short introductory statement will be quite obvious. However, it may make your business sound like an 'also ran'. You may just sound like the twenty-eighth company in your industry. So, what sets you apart from everyone else? What is your USP (Unique Selling Proposition)? This is a good start.

Now, take your elevator pitch and see if it sounds like it's adding value. What I mean by that is does it sound like something I can't do without?

If your pitch is something like, "We provide a full range of supplies and accessories for all domestic home building projects", that may sound impressive but it doesn't set you apart from the next company that does the same thing. Try, "We save builders time and money by carrying local stock of everything they need to complete a home building project". Instantly we can see the difference. It's the same company but we have added a statement of value right at the front, 'Save time and money'.

Have a play around with your own elevator pitch and see how convincing and value-driven it can sound.

The next step is to list the benefits you believe are strong contenders for the top ten benefits of your company, its products or services. You may want to do this as a team or small group – get the input from everyone that has a vested interest.

With that list, take each one and expand the reasons for that benefit. This is the, 'So What?' technique we talked about earlier. If you need reminding, flip back a few pages. This is where you keep asking the question, 'So what?' to the benefit you've listed. This helps to see how much real value it is.

The next step is to look at your list of benefits and their actual values and pick the key benefit – the thing that sets you apart from everyone else. You may care to have a look at your elevator pitch again. Does it include this key benefit? Is this key benefit the same as your listed USP or is there an opportunity to change it?

Remember, this key benefit may be the most obvious one to you but it may not be the one thing for all your customers. However, it's a really good start because you have identified ten really good benefits and drilled down to real value (cost savings, time benefits or some other form or hard measurable benefit) and you've identified the key benefit that you feel, overall, sums up what makes you unique.

Now, the final step here is to take a look at some of your customers, or potential customers, and link their needs to the benefits you have listed. Or start the other way round and see who you think can really benefit from what you have to offer.

Keep the paper you have written all this on, type it up and keep it with you, learn it and refine it. This is the essence of your company offering.

You may have convinced yourself that what you have is now unbeatable in the market place. People will still have some objections however and you will need to be prepared for them. You'll see what I mean when you read through the next chapter.

Objections

Objection handling is one of the key salesperson techniques to develop. Having answers to those objections ready and handy is good preparation. Building answers to likely objections in the presentation will head them off before they even surface.

Price

Using ROI as an approach will also reduce the number of discount requests customers raise. By showing the ROI model, you remove the need to discuss discounts because you are already showing the customer the return they will be getting for your product or service. If you are showing a return in a reasonable timeframe, they are probably not even thinking about a discount because they can see the financial benefits in front of them. If they are thinking about a discount, they are unlikely to bring it up because it will just seem greedy. In essence ROI methodology helps your customers see that your price has little to do with costs and a lot more to do with the value you deliver. In fact ROI based selling can reduce the sales cycle time drastically because people won't want to wait to start reaping the benefits. How long would you want to wait if your grocery bill could be cut in half the minute you started shopping somewhere else. Or would it take you long to sign up to a new supplier if it meant that your electricity bill would be 40% cheaper?

Delay in decision

When you show a valid ROI argument to a customer you are helping them see that the longer they delay, the more money they are losing. When store owners are engaged in building their stores they know that every week of delay in opening they lose out on potential sales. Likewise, if you have shown in your ROI the amount of cost savings or new sales they can receive from using your product or service, then the longer they delay, the less they will see of those benefits.

This is not something you have to push too hard as they can see it for themselves. If someone said to you, we'll start covering all of your fuel bills the minute you tell us to, how long would it take you to go ahead? Try and get used to showing the ROI benefits in that way to help create a sense of urgency without pushing.

Don't believe it

This is a common objection. Some people will not want to go ahead without some proof. What you will need here is either a guarantee of some sort to take away the risk for the customer or some references or case studies to show how it's worked elsewhere. If you're not keen on the guarantee idea (why wouldn't you be if you stand behind your product?) then get some data to support your claims. If you don't have any, go back to former customers and get some. Ask them questions like, "How has our product or service impacted on your business? Have your costs reduced as a result?" If so, by how much? How do you attribute this to our product or service? Make it easy for them and be prepared. Ask them some questions that will be easy for them to answer or offer to help gather the information needed.

Be armed with a few case studies, figures to back up what you claim. It also helps as part of your presentation to talk about a few of the successes you have had and name the clients. You can draw comparisons to the current customer to show an even closer fit to the product or service you are offering. You could say, "ABC Company are also in your industry and they have a similar sized workforce. They were a little sceptical at first but after just one month, they noticed a marked improvement." Or "XYZ International are a pretty demanding organisation. They decided to go ahead after they saw the short term payback. They would be more than happy to tell you of their success with this service."

Already have a supplier

We talked about incumbents earlier. Incumbents are even trickier to negotiate if they are friends with the customer or even worse – related. Sometimes, no matter what you do, people won't change. You could offer stuff for free and that wouldn't be enough. However, sometimes people are just comfortable or think it will be too hard to change. These are great candidates to use this approach on. Remember, you are showing them good reason to change. Help them see the logical argument for your product or service. It's true that people make emotional purchases but people also make logical purchases – remember the 'no brainer'? Buying a product or service as a 'no brainer' has long lasting effect. Emotional purchases often lead to buyer's remorse. Admit it, we've all made purchases on an emotional impulse and even when we're handing over the money we can start to feel the doubts kick in!

A lot of the time, there will already be a current supplier in place, so get used to having it come up as an objection. Better still, head it off at the start by saying something like, "I know you probably already have a supplier for this and they've probably provided you with real value. Let me show you how we can extend that value for you and improve your financial position." Notice we haven't knocked the current supplier. If we knock them, we also knock our customer for choosing them in the first place. It's best always to keep the supplier on side by helping them save face. Confirm they have made good decisions up till now. You may go as far as saying that up until you could offer what you have today, the choice they made was the best option available.

Help them see that although they have a good relationship with their current supplier it makes good business sense to take advantage of what you have to offer. Work on logic rather than emotion in these cases.

Link to business objectives

You want to make it easy for your customer to make a decision and buy your product or service. One sure way to help them and the rest of the company get on board is to link the benefits of choosing your offering to their business objectives or drivers. If your benefits include improving the safety of their staff and one of the company drivers is to reduce accidents in the workplace – marry it up! If they are keen to increase profitability (who isn't?) and your offering will increase profits, show them the link.

This may sound simple but make sure you point all these things out. Believe it or not, this all sounds so simple everybody should already know it right? Wrong! Remember the part in the introduction about me pitching this idea to the worldwide electronics firm? People just aren't using this approach. It's almost as if they haven't seen the link. And again, even if everyone started using it, there's plenty of room to improve your version and hone in on the benefits for that particular customer.

You could apply this same thinking to your own purchases. When you buy something is it helping to contribute to your goals and objectives? Try it in your company. Ask questions when a purchase is being considered. How does this link to our strategy or our vision? The more we think this way, the more we see a connection between what we do and what we focus on – and by focus I mean energy, money and thinking time. If we don't have a clear vision or clear objectives, we often have sporadic habits of spending and, to put it kindly, eclectic views on just about everything.

Summary

Success in your sales role depends on a lot more than showing features and benefits. It relies on you being able to translate those benefits into tangible financial metrics that illustrate the real value of your product or service versus that of your competitors.

Competitors to you may not just be the people in your industry. Nowadays, budgets are being cut and exchanged across multiple departments. What was once a training budget is now being used to buy new computers. Marketing may lose out to software enhancements. You need to have convincing arguments across budget channels. In fact, if you can show how someone can create a budget out of the savings you'll be helping them make, you can create your own sales opportunities.

The sales cycle time is likely to be greatly reduced when you can show a reasonable ROI because it is showing the customer the cost of delay. The longer they wait the more money they are wasting. Here you can create some tension for the customer. Help them see that it's crazy to put off the decision. Remember that over half of sales decisions are delayed and that most of those never result into a sale. Work on convincing the customer that waiting to make a decision is making them out of pocket. Remember the following:

- Know your company's key benefits and that of the products or services you offer.

- Take time to work out the value of the key benefits as they are likely to be translated into dollars for most of your customers.

- Know your competitors and how you stack up against them.

Most people buy for emotional reasons – a connection or belief in the story behind the product. It's hard to compete with that, especially if emotionally your offering doesn't stack up, such as against a long relationship with an incumbent. Providing a convincing ROI argument creates a logical purchasing position for the customer. Logical positions are stronger and longer lasting than emotional ones because you can't argue with facts. Get away from opinions and stick with the facts. Make them black and white and show the customer that the right choice is the one you have illustrated will give them the greatest benefit.

Be ready with case studies or references to back up your claims. Have a trial period or guarantee available if it's possible. Give them every reason to go ahead and no reason to say no.

Good luck in your sales role. If you have found this book to be useful, I'd love to hear from you.

Derek Good Bio

Derek is an author, actor, presenter, facilitator, voice over artist, husband, father of four children and currently a director of LearningPlanet Limited which helps improve the productivity of organisations and the confidence of their staff through sales, service and leadership skills in bite-sized videos and short training modules.

Derek is a facilitator who works with leadership teams in LEGO Serious Play, TMI profiling, problem solving and strategy sessions.

As a director of LearningPlanet – a worldwide content developer of videos in soft skills available on a standalone platform and for embedding on learning management systems, he is responsible for spearheading customer relationships programmes and manages all the sales and communications functions for the business.

Derek has over twenty years' experience in general management in the UK and New Zealand market, is an Author of several books on leadership, coaching, sales, Return on investment, training activities and humour. He has also been a past winner in the Westpac Enterprise Auckland North Shore Business Excellence Awards and the TUANZ innovation award for Education.

Other books available from Derek Good

101 Training Activities and How to Run Them by Derek Good & Craig McFadyen

Paperback & Kindle: 254 pages

First Published: 2018

ISBN-10: 1987708784
ISBN-13: 978-1987708783

Practical Leadership by Derek Good

Paperback & Kindle: 172 pages

First Published: 2015

ISBN-10: 1512311650

ISBN-13: 978-1512311655

Leading a Team by Derek Good

Paperback: 104 pages
First Published: 2012
ISBN-13: 978-1478332039
ISBN-10: 1478332034

Coaching and Feedback Made Easy by Derek Good

Paperback: 82 pages
First Published: 2010
ISBN-10: 1453844384
ISBN-13: 978-1453844380

Return on Investment Made Easy by Derek Good & Craig McFadyen

Paperback: 108 pages

First Published: 2010

ISBN-10: 1452835993

ISBN-13: 978-1452835990